The Healing Quest Publishing
Www.thehealingquest.com

Contact & order information:
Websites: www.empowerpuzzles.com
            www.thehealingquest.com
Email: thehealingquest@hotmail.com
Facebook: Kate.ellis19
Facebook Words that Empower ~ URL; /mindful.puzzles
Facebook: Anxiety and Depression is not a life sentence ~ URL; /youareunlimited
Facebook: /The Healing Quest

Because of the dynamic nature of the Internet, any Web addresses or links contained in this book may have changed since publication and may be no longer valid. The views expressed in this work are solely those of the author and do not necessarily reflect the views of the publisher, and the publisher hereby disclaims any responsibility for them.

ISBN: 978-0-9850483-7-2

The author of this book does not dispense medical advice or prescribe the use of any techniques as a form of treatment for physical, emotional, or medical problems without the advice of a physician, either directly or indirectly. The intent of the author is only to offer information of a general nature to help you in your quest for emotional and spiritual well-being. In the event you use any of the information in this book for yourself, which is your constitutional right, the author and the publisher assume no responsibility for your actions.

November 2011

Printed in the United States of America.

Acknowledgements

It is with great gratitude I thank Yvonne Balala, who left a purple transparent folder on my bed with a note stating: "Are you ever gonna do *something* with this?"

This book was written originally in the 1990's, put aside and buried. Thanks to Linda Randall for reviews and critiques, and being my best friend.

This is for you, Reader, may you find peace through Knowledge. You are an unending horizon.

Kate Ellis

"Did You Know" by Kate Ellis provides a simple pathway of learning about how the thought/feeling/emotion/belief processes of our minds work. She gently guides the reader with educational steps on how to take charge of our mind - the reward being a more peaceful and balanced state of being. She concludes her guide with fun techniques on maintaining a focused, quiet space that strengthens our ability to clearly focus and relax our mind in the present. A delightful read with wisdom for everyone!

Triza Schultz, author of the book, "The Fear Standard - A Guide And Personal Journey To Regain Our Intuitive Spirit"

Kate has beautifully and poetically composed the simple truths of self-mastery. Artistically written, Kate has created a readable hypnotic journey sure to transform how you think...therefore how you feel. I highly recommend "Did You Know?" to be your constant pocket or purse companion....certain to be your loving reminder of your perpetual creatorship.

Michelle Lee, CH
Founder of Athena Rising Now a program dedicated to freeing teens girls, their mothers, and all women from ancient cultural programming to become the leaders they were born to be. www.AthenaRisingNow.com

Kate Ellis is able to convey a plethora of wisdoms that have been passed down through the centuries.
Kate's style is rather poetic, and like most good poetry it instills thought.... sometimes deep thoughts..
You stand to be commended, and I would definitely recommend this read to anyone.

Rod Kelly, BCH.
Board Certified Consulting Hypnotist

When I started reading "Did You Know," I immediately thought of Eckhart Tolle and "Power of Now" and how much better Kate Ellis' little book is, especially in a practical way. Mind you, this is just after reading a page.

How did I know? Mostly because I know Kate Ellis fairly well and I took a bit of time to investigate Mr. Tolle when I first looked at his work.
It is my habit to study the author's background and motivations to evaluate

better what I am reading, especially when the material is presumed to be important for a person's life.

And what is more important than a person's life? Not the author's life so much, but your life as reader, which the author's work is supposed to help enhance. I believe that reading is not just about having some awareness, but more about getting real results.

The image that comes to mind in comparing "Did You Know" with "Power of Now" is that of swimming in deep waters versus stepping through a shallow pond. As you can imagine they are very different experiences and each has its own value and reward.

It appears that Tolle wrote and worked his book to become a popular spiritual author. He succeeded in that.

When it comes to Kate's little book, it seems that she wrote it for herself as much as for anybody else. She didn't tell me this; I am inferring, and of course I may be wrong. What I know about Kate is that she is a serious person who at times will do the work and always strives to do her best for her clients.

What I come away with in reading "Did You Know" is Kate's own struggles in thinking hard about the connections among thoughts, emotions and feelings and how they affect our lives. She is presenting us with her findings at the point in time that she was writing.

Because Kate can think deeply, "Did You Know" offers considerable value... if you are willing to do the work, learn about yourself and extract the value. The book is brief. There are many pages with one or two ideas, and others with a set of words and phrases. I want to emphasize that because it is why this book can be more valuable for you.

This is a book that you need to carry around with a notebook (paper or electronic), and then you read and re-read and write (or dictate.) You will get a lot of value, not because you agree with the material, but because you use it as a foil to arrive at your own conclusions.

For me, that is why Kate's "Did You Know" has more practical importance than most best-selling books relating to self-growth and personal development.
Jim Namaste

Introduction

Contained within the pages of this simple book is an intro-
duction on how the mind, thoughts, feelings and emotions
work with and through each other. Specifically, within this
material we dive into the heart of operations creating external
consciousness, how personal perceptions build a foundation
of personal reality. How we think and then in turn feel con-
cerning our personal selves is directly related to our experiences in life. How we perceive, conceive through our personal beliefs is a measure of success or failure one experiences in a life. It is of great importance we continue to look
and expand ideas of personal reality. Our beliefs, feelings
and mostly the emotions that underlie the currents, the motion and direction emotion points the thought process.

It is not that one allows emotions to undermine portions of
the self; what we think and assess to whom and what we are,
our value as a person but one does not heed the require-
ments and opportunities emotion provides.
Emotions, messengers of the true self; That honest aspect of
self that experiences, reacts and acknowledges feelings and
thoughts without the awkwardness of the ego to raise its pro-
tective defenses.
Messenger of the soul (emotion): That portion that acknowledges the essence of balance or imbalance. Emotion
emerges from the depths within to deliver information, to
create or return a mind to a semblance of wholism, centered-
ness, of harmony.

Ignorance is the heartbreaker, but fear is the mind killer.
Heeding such messages from and through the emotions re-
turns control and responsibility to the individual.

By choosing not to respond to these messages one locks aspects of the entirety of self, our emotions, mental outlook, physical health and spiritual growth including the growth in becoming a fully functional human being into a state of suspension.

You get what you concentrate on.
Whether it is a specific focus of an imaged goal or that of scatteredness, simply going along. With scatteredness one achieves a hodgepodge of experience, a literal grab-bag of information, of environments and responses from others with varying degrees of personal response/reactions and perspective from where you stand. Ever believe no one understands you? This is how it is created.

Know thy self.
You are shadow and light, each an aspect dependant upon the other. Each aspect of self balances creating a momentum of a cycle of growth, understanding and expansion mentally, physically and spiritually. Each aspect of ourselves invaluable to the expansion and development of a whole self.
The shadow aspect of the personality is not a perversion of the light aspect, nor an undesirable...More so a compliment, a creative component of an individual personality. What is a painting without the assistance of varying light and dark...It creates richness, depth...A certain type of reality that make sense to the perceiver and the concepts brought through and by the viewing.

Chapter One

Did you know....

The mind can only hold one (1) thought at a time?

The buzzing noise you may hear in your ear is the

Whoosh!

Of rapid thoughts bouncing....................

Thoughts stack themselves one upon another, like a sandwich or layer cake. It feels as though you are bombarded by hundreds/thousands/millions of ideas and memories and thought of futures, sometimes with images, sounds, feelings, smells, even tastes..................

You can begin to notice and observe that all of these thoughts have something in common...

Similar to a story, there is a thread that connects and runs through thought, that keeps them in a type of order, like one frame of film follows another in a continuity or feelings that compound...

Did you know your mind is a tool...

Like a hammer or doorknob or
paintbrush.

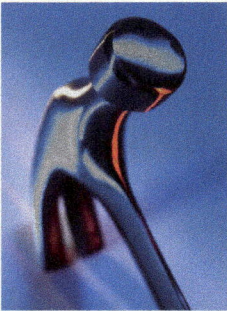

How you use your tool of a mind will be a direct result of the amount of control you have...

...or don't

Your mind is a feed-back system. It takes commands from in-put that your thoughts think, image......

Through any of the five senses.

If you awake in the morning and look outside the window and notice it is a cloudy day (and you don't like cloudy, dark dank days), you may find yourself thinking; "I hate cloudy dark days, it's going to be a dismal day!"

....OR.....................................

The thought might be so rapid you do not catch yourself thinking it! Your mind will also take commands from your body language, like a frown or a smile or holding your head down.

Whether you are conscious of it or not, you have given a command or directive to your mind (subconscious) and it will unquestioningly do as you ask... It will be a bad day.

You are always giving direction to your mind.
With every thought.
In the way you use and hold your body.
Through thoughts you continue to feel.

Your control or power is always in the present!

!!!!!!!!!!!!!!!!!!!!!!!!!!!!!!!!!!!!!! NOW !!!!!!!!!!!!!!!!!!!!!!!!!!!!!!!!!!!!

Your mind can only respond and react to commands that are thought in the present moment.

Where you are right now, in the NOW, the present is WHERE you begin every moment. This means you have a CHOICE to THINK or REACT to current thought, images, memories, prediction, feelings and ideas, past, present.

NOT
 THEN
   WHEN
      PAST
        AGO

Childhood
     Teenage-hood
          Yesterday.................

Not Tomorrow, Later, Future, Soon,
Ahead, Plans, Dreams, Hopes.

You can begin to notice that your thoughts
have something in common................
They are very similar in arrangement, like fear-
ful thoughts.

Fear feeds fear!
The thought or context, fear, will generate
other LIKE thoughts, remembrances. The
mind will pull up other things that go under the
heading: Fear.

Like a filing system, the mind accesses anything
related to what you want to know, even if you
didn't know you wanted to know this stuff!

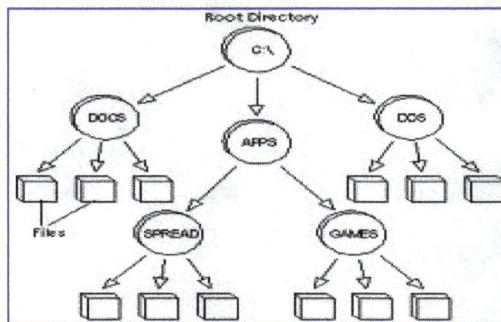

Now take another look, and observe what is
similar to the line of thinking you were sorting
through.

ONLY your thoughts can travel through time....

By thinking of the past or future you are actually time traveling! You can confirm this by noticing that your physical body reacts to thought events...

Like if you imagine a favorite vacation spot; Your body begins to relax, feeling pleasure... You can feel on a varied scale: The temperature, sounds, sights, tastes.....

.... OR ....

Remembering the past, perhaps not so fun times, abuses or failures. You can notice your body tense up, feelings change that do not make sense with your current reality, what is around you. You can see, hear, taste and feel what was....

Your
Mind
Is
A-maze-ing!

Your mind is here (NOW).
You are here.
NOW, in the present.
Your thoughts may be other-where,
you can draw your thoughts back. Here!
You are the master of your mind.
But to master your mind, you need to be in the
Now.

To confirm you are here, in the present moment look into a mirror; Observe the environment around you.
Touch one hand to the other.
Notice how solidly you are anchored here!

The best way to draw attention to the here and
now is to take a deep breath, hold it for a second and then release it in a slow, controlled
blow.

When you draw in the air around you,
the oxygen saturates every muscle, every tendon and the tissues throughout your body. It
also relaxes, refreshes and gently stimulates
your brain by delivering rich nutrient filled
oxygen.

Now... Find where your thoughts are!
Encourage...
Bring them back, here, now.

You may have to search in many different
places, spaces of time. As you bring your attention back to the present, you may notice how
spacious it truly is. A lot of time the present
seems confining, tight and compact.

But, as you breathe, your thoughts will slow
down, until you become aware that you are
thinking or concentrating on only a few things
or feelings or objects in your immediate environment

YOU'RE BACK!

You have power.
You have control.
But
In
Only One
Place...

The present moment.

You have power.
You have control.
But
In
Only
One
Time...

The present moment.

Fear, or any other emotion like guilt, hurt feelings, anger, jealousy cannot live in the now.

Think about it.
ALL OF THESE EMOTIONS are based in another time frame. If you are not being threatened by another person, or a tiger or speeding car heading for you while crossing the street, you are accessing from the past or future or both
Combined.

Fear feeds from memory
                Thoughts of past
                            Of future.

Fear needs the oxygen of thoughts.

Like fire...
Fire needs a place to burn.
Fire needs food, oxygen.

Take these things essential to fire away,
and fire goes away.
It cannot exist.

Everything in life, as we know it has
"ground rules."
The basics of life are to have shelter, food, wa-
ter and reproduce. Another important element
is love.

Love of self and/or others.

Your thoughts are fuel.
Each thought is oxygen...
Stop thought...

Stop, slow thoughts until you have only a few.
You can pay attention to your environment.
You can focus on your breath.
You can listen to a song on the radio.
You can listen to some of the noises around you.

You cannot completely Stop thought.
What you are actually doing is slowing down the speed.
You shall notice that each thought FOLLOWS another.
Like ducklings in a row.
Even though the ducklings came from the same mother, each is independent, it's own duck-self.

You are the master of your mind.

You are the only master of your mind.
But you can only master your mind by being in the present.

It does not matter how long it takes to accomplish bringing back all of your thoughts, ideas, memories, hopes, wishes.... Back.
You do not give up or abandon your thoughts.
Your thoughts will always be there to think as long as you want them.

It does not matter how much you slow
Thought.
It matters that you have.
You are in control.
You are always in control.

You are not always in control of your
Environment.
You are not in control of the people around
You.

You can only control yourself.
You can only control your feelings.
You can only slow down the pace of thought.

Try it!
Do it!
Think only one thought...

Pick something...........................Now.

Think of one thing...

It could be listening to the radio, pick an instrument to focus your attention like a guitar, bass, drums, violin, piano.
OR
Reading a book, paper, cereal box.
OR
Looking at a rain drop
         Snowflake
         Cloud
         Cream in your coffee......................

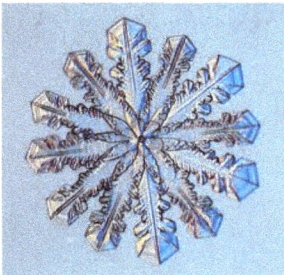

As you focus your mind on a thought,
Look,
Listen,
Observe.

Do not follow your thoughts.
They may want to take you to other places!
Because they are so interesting!
You may even discover new thoughts,
perhaps some that were too quick for you to
catch before...

Look, Listen, Observe......................Only!

That is your thought.......................Focus.

Every time thoughts come to say;
"this is stupid!"
Say; "Yes it is..."

And then return to your one thought focus.

You are the mater of your mind.
Like a mother who has not disciplined her children, they may run around,
not listen,
or pay attention to her calls to come home.

Or like a bunch of marbles placed on a flat table, they may want to roll around, off the edges to the ground.
You may have to find a bowl or place or block of some sort to keep them all together.

Your thoughts may want to run wild, even faster than before.
You may feel as though you are chasing them around,
and around,
and around and around!

Pretend you are standing still; let them come back to you.
Gently, patiently call them back.

Every time a thought comes up to comment,
say, "Okay!"

Your thoughts are there.
A lot of the time they are valid in what they are
saying.

Now, back to your one thought...

And do this over and
            Over
        And over
            Over and
        And Over
            Over and
        And Over
            Over and
            Over

Your stray thoughts **WILL** run out of ideas to
distract you.
Your stray thoughts, the ones you do not pay
attention to, if it is not your one thought focus,
from whatever you picked **WILL** run out of
criticisms, excuses, put-downs.
Your stray thoughts **WILL** become bored,
shall become tired, exhausted from all that
running around!

Your thoughts **WILL** stop fighting!
Your thoughts **WILL** begin to realize that they
are not being brushed aside...Because when a
thought grabs your attention, and you say;
"YES! I know you are there, but you need to
rest for a while," it will know that you are not
abandoning thoughts, just slowing them down.

And then MAGIC happens!

You are thinking only one thought!

It may be a few seconds at a time.
It may be a fraction of a second.
But it doesn't matter HOW long...
It matters that you did it!
You are in control,
in the moment...
Where your power resides, lives, exists.
Your power is in the present moment.
You are the master of your mind.

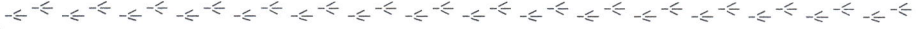

And then MAGIC happens!

You are not feeling good or bad.........................

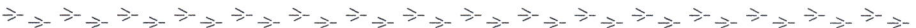

Experience the Magic!
Notice; observe the power of thinking just one
thought.

You are focused.
Attention on your one thought.

Not focused on feelings
                    Judgments
                    Opinions
                    Conceptions
                    Ideals
                    Hopes
                    Wishes
                    Pain
                    Hurt
                    Boredom
                    Decisions
                    Success....................................

Chapter Two

THOUGHTS CREATES FEELINGS.

And with only one thought you are just here.
In the present.
In the moment.
In the now.

Feelings come from memory; memory are
thoughts, images, ideas, beliefs and experiences; they are in the past
Time frame.

The future is not here. It's time frame is again
different from past and present. Ideas about
the future and thought projections from your
accumulated experiences based in the past and
Present, in time.

Mr. Andy Hauck asked; "Can you show me ten
minutes from now?
Can you show me ten minutes ago?"

All you really have is the present moment,
now!

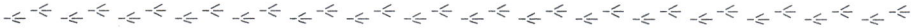

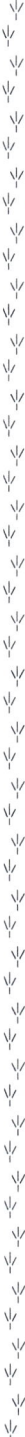

Your mind will fight!
But that is okay.............

You may need to teach your mind new thoughts.
Human beings like what is familiar.
The familiar is something known.
You know what to expect, even if you do not like what you get, it feels safe for the most part.

Feeling safe is important.
That is why you may have become trapped by the familiar.
It is a type of control, being trapped.

Thoughts and time are a team:
Past = When
 Present = Now
                Your
                Point
                Of
                Power
Future = Possibilities.

Old, safe feeling thoughts will say; "I'm not in control anymore...
Power."

That is a valid thought.
It is okay.
You, yourself is safe.
It is old thought that fears for it's 'life'.
It is true you may either have to drop an old friendly thought because it does not suit you any further, or perhaps it has become too limiting/confining.

You may be able to expand on the original limiting thought. Do not push away or blow off your thoughts. Give them time, you have been giving and entertaining certain thoughts for a long time. When you push something or somebody away, they will push back harder, not accepting refusal of your attentions.

Like children; If you fail to pay attention to them and give them some of your time, they will do anything to get your attention! If they do something good, and you do not recognize their efforts, the child will try another approach. If the child does something wrong, or destructive and you yell at them, that is attention!

Even though you yelled and probably screamed, they felt recognized. And will continue the same behavior that provoked a response.

Some thoughts are so familiar, they feel like family. They become a part of you. You thought them, nurtured them by giving your focus and attentions, feed them with more thoughts that were similar and comfy. You in essence raise these thoughts to where they are now.

Just like children; They may not know the reason they are mis-behaving for attention... They, those unwanted thoughts only know they are being validated. They can feel their existence.

You, your conscious thinking mind is the Power.

Consciously choosing your thoughts can be challenging.
It's like physical exercise, if you haven't done it in a while, your body will be sore.

But you can accept that.
It happens.

If a physical routine becomes too difficult, it is wise to slow down, or find another program more suited to your needs, style and taste.

As you are exercising choice of thought, your mind may also get sore...
But you can accept that.
It happens!

Expect some challenge, be persistent, be gentle with you.

Just as your body becomes used to the new routine, so will your mind.
Just as your body is prone to being flexible, so is your mind.
Your mind is actually more flexible than your body.
Your body is limited in many ways.
There are no limits to the mind!

As you begin to use all the muscles forgotten in your body, you shall also discover new muscles in your thinking mind.

You will begin to feel good and strong!
The discomforts
     Dissipates
     Diminish
     Dissolve
     Disappears
     Retreats
     Relaxes
     Relinquishes
     Releases any and all grips it may have had.

In Body, In Mind, In All ways.

New and strange things begin to happen...
Feelings change.
Fear becomes excitement...
Fear does not feel exactly the same...
Fear seems to have a choice to it now.
And it does.
As you change your thoughts about fear, you
change your feelings...

Remember: Thoughts create feelings.

Other feelings change also, as you think about them.
When you attempt to avoid these thoughts that creates the feelings, they become stronger, the exact thing you try to avoid!

Anxiety becomes anticipation...
Sadness becomes equal to the past (time frame)

Hope becomes commitment.
Pain becomes courage.
Anger becomes energy (energy to change).
Guilt transforms, as you allow, into forgiveness
Of
Self
Others
Both.

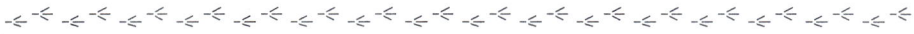

And, seemingly all of a sudden...
A big, apparent insurmountable problem,
becomes incredibly simple!

All complications were only thoughts!
Feeding upon one another!

Only a thought...
How powerful!

Look how powerful you are!
You think and choose thought.
How simple.

And since all thoughts share something similar,
if you pay attention and focus on either your
feelings or the thread of sameness that runs
through your thoughts, you can change at will
whatever you are focusing on...
By breath or sight or sound or anything that
exists in the present moment.

Thoughts and feelings seemed to have a life of their own. But now that you know the process of how you work, you can assume ownership of you again.

It is okay to forget or have forgotten you are in control of you.
Sometimes we are not taught these important facts of life.
Sometimes our elders who raised us were not aware.
Sometimes they put their faith in things other than themselves.
Sometimes they blame luck, having it or not having it.
Sometimes they blame God for what they have or don't.
Sometimes they blamed others for being responsible for anything and everything.

It is okay if you have forgotten, or blamed or displaced responsibility.
We are human.
We are learning.
We are flexible.
We are capable.
We can only do our best with what we have or know in the present moment.

We are more than human-beings, we are
Humans-becoming.
We are always in the process of becoming
more than we were. Even if it's just old.
There is always a progress.
It may be fast.
It may be slow.
But what matters is that it is happening.

Not realizing or recognizing we are doing the
thinking,
choosing
continuing.

The thought process/progress itself is a matter
of knowledge.
Knowledge is power.
You can choose to own it.
You can choose to abandon it.
Sometimes we choose both.

Claim your power.
Choose a thought.
Now observe how you feel...

You have just created a feeling.
Was it happiness
                    Sadness
                        Comfort
                            Anxiousness
                            Lightness
                            Heaviness
                            Balance...?

Thoughts and feelings are like children, like
people: They are not comfortable being alone
for long periods of time.

We are by nature social animals.
Some of us need more attention and company
of other people. It helps us feel a safety within.
There are also some people that only need the
company and attentions of others once in a
while.

What both of these types of people have in
common is that they need others.

Some people want to be part of a group, want-
ing to help, support and be supported.
Then there are some that do not want to be a
part of a group, just know that they are still
accepted.

Like attracts like...
Physical law,
Universal law.

The same laws apply to the thought process
and progress.

Similar thoughts attract
Same type
Thought
And
Feeling
And
Attitude
And health
And wellness
And balance

You choose or intend a thought on a subject,
and that sets up the format or foundation of
other
like-thought–forms.

Through you intention, attentions you create,
control and empower the process and progress.

The feeling of being bombarded by thoughts is
really your feelings of being overwhelmed by
the rapid swirling, tangling of thought and idea.
Since thoughts gravitate to each other, each
thought 'backs up' the other thoughts.
Each thought builds upon, strengthens the
structure of thoughts and ideas right before it...

You are very powerful!
You are creative!
You can build a mountain with the smallest of thought/idea.
You are in control!
Your mountain can be full of life, growth, greenery.
Or it can be a desert, desolate, alone.

Chapter Three

Have you noticed we are in a world filled with people?

There is a reason for this...

We need each other!
Especially in these times and moments we exist
in,
Live in.

We need each other to be born
                    Help
                    Hurt
                    Heal
                    Aggravate
                    Love
                    Disappoint
                    Hold......................

We need one another so we don't get lonely
and die, or become bored.
Have you ever taken stock, noticed people in
your life, environment, and the ones you hang
around with?

Have you become aware of how these others
Reflects to you those things that you love the
most, or hate...

Have you ever wondered why?!
Have you been blaming luck?
Have you ever considered there may be a very
good reason for those nearest to you...?

Have you yet noticed that there is a reason for
everything?

Could those people be reflecting you?
A clear distinct you not recognized before?
You are so close to you, it can be hard to back
up and see a clear true image.
Like, those others can be reflecting, as a mirror
an image... Not an exact duplicate...
For you are an individual.
There are no Others exactly like you.
Never was...

...Never will be.
You are the original model.

Others reflect you symbolically, your likes and
Dislikes...
Things you admire, things you despise.

How can you have Feeling for things that are
not within yourself, as a working model or potential?
We are speaking of those in your life, environment.
Not those on t.v.
In newspapers.
Those whom you have no personal contact
with.

What if your personal environment is a sym-
bolic reflect of whom and what you truly are?

All peoples of the world have created humor!
It exists in every country, land, cultures.

Humor helps us to deal with others and our reactions to them: they're weirdness, as well as
our own.

Are there those who humor you?
By being themselves...
Can they help but BE themselves?
Can YOU but help be yourself?
If you can laugh at and with others, you can laugh at and with yourself.

Humor heals, restores balance, and creates commonalities.
Humor releases internal thought grips and opens a space for expansion, expansion of self Awareness.
Gently, fully.

Yet... We are all strangers in a strange world....

...But all related....
A paradox!

When we cannot see our own reflections,
when we forget our gift of humor we can feel
disconnected.

That happens from judgments.
On self or others.

As individual as each and every one of us are,
so must judgment of self, situation, people be.
If judgments are not expansive and inclusive to
an individual or event or people, it can become
quite dangerous,
for them, us, all!

Even justice systems look at individual cases.
Sometimes new laws are made to expand and
include all aspects, probabilities and situations.

Again, there is a unique-ness to each and every
thing.
Even if appearances smack of similarities.
A closer look, or stepping back can open views
not fully seen.

WATCH! Pay attention to your thoughts....
They are always judging
                    Analyzing
                    Evaluating
Self, others and thought thunk.

Our judgments state whether some thing, body,
self, is good or bad.

Just as people feel there are safety in numbers, as like being in a crowd or group of others... That is what thoughts do and speak through an un-trained, mis-used mind.

REMEMBER! We gravitate towards the familiar. It feels safe, comfy and in it's own way, sincere.

The mind gets used to bunches
                    Clutches
                    Gaggles
                    Groups
                    Bundles
                    Schools
                    Packs
                    Clusters
                    Collections
                    Crowds
                              of thoughts.

Your feelings are a direct result from
Thought...
Thought
Creates
Feelings
Feelings
Draws Emotion
Emotion = motion of thought and feeling
Combined.

...Current thought...

You cannot feel from a thought thunk
Yesterday
Last night
One hour ago...

...Only on what is being chewed on now...

You react (emotion) on judgment created during the original thought process (idea).
That is why it may seem as though your feelings are continued through time.
Actually, you re-create a feeling every time you
access a thought that is familiar, like seeing a
person you know very well, like a family
member...Even as time may shift and shape
their appearance, you can recognize easily who
they are.

Technically speaking; When you think and feel
a thought you create a neuronal path-way in
your brain, like a trail or roadway you use a lot.
You can easily recognize it and know instantly
where you are. If you use this 'roadway' a lot,
you take for granted that it is there. Never
questioning if it will be there tomorrow, or even
sometimes where it came from.

This is sometimes referred to as a Habit.
Like a groove, you easily fall into it, not always
realizing you have just gotten onto an old familiar road, trail, brain path-way.

If you are in this moment depressed
Saddened
Anxious
Panicked
Happy
Worried
Pleased
Balanced, that is a
creation of yours!

You may have forgotten!
You are the master of your mind,
Creator!

Automatically you recall, react to attached
Feelings = emotions.

It seems as though these things JUST happen...

And it did!

That is the wonderful thing about you...
You continually create reactions to thoughts,
Perception.

And you create/recreate your feelings...
...In every moment...

But your thoughts and feelings may feel as old
as the hills,
because of a "programmed" reaction
(motion of emotion)
to a thought-idea.

But it is only a C O N T I N U A T I O N of
the same type of...

...You know!

T
H
O
U
G
H
T

Perceptions
Conceptions
Ideas
Reactions
Conclusions
Decisions
Ideals

They are like old friends our habitual thoughts.
And they ARE!
They have comforted us.
They have scared us.
They have healed us.
They have wounded us.

What is your steak (or veggie)?
What is your poison?

You can decide.

You choose your likes and dislikes.
You decide what is tolerable.

You choose and decide by what "tastes" good or feels good.
That is how you know/judge.
But remember; Knowing and judging is based on "past",
Experience.

Are you THINKING or REACTING?
Are your thoughts befriending or betraying
you?

If you are THINKING about your thoughts or
situations or people around, you are living in
the present...
You are using all resources available currently
from the past and present to respond.

If you are REACTING to your thoughts or
situations or people around, you are riding the
currents of the past.
With the singular focus on the past time frame,
you cut off potential and abilities to expand
your MIND to people, places and things.

You are using the old familiar 'path-way."

You are not your thoughts!

You just pick and choose them, thoughts...
Hold them or release them.
As well as feelings that they create or emotions
that are already attached...
Or did you forget?

Do you have a place or chair or couch or side of the bed that is yours?
Your space...
Is it comfortable when it is being used by another?

Your mind will feel/act the same way, with the same level of comfort or discomfort...
Through thoughts
            Perceptions
            Ideas
            Conclusions
            Ideals
            Judgments
            Conditions
        The comfort zone

Until the mind gets used to new—ways of thought.

When you change some-thing, it can be
Uncomfortable.
Like when someone uses your space, place.
Expect a period of adjustment!

It could be the same amount of time it took to
get to where you are now...
For many people 21 days to a month is the
period of time it takes to get used to a new
way...

Like using a new road or path or thought.
When a person moves to a new home,
it commonly takes 21 days to get used to the
new environment, used to ways to get to and
from home and back.

Change can be as uncomfortable as the old way
was.
The benefit of a new way; an expansion, is a
betterment, harmony, balance, knowledge,
power, control and understanding.

A period of adjustment means that you can begin to get used too...it does not mean the **CHANGE** is done, only started.

Like when you begin to walk a new path in a familiar park, you may become ultra-aware of sights, sounds, people, places and things.
Your senses are wide open.
You use senses more precisely.
They aren't the same old senses in a sense...
Now the twist of discovery is present, and YOU are present,
Really present.

Be patient!
That is rule #1...

Rule #2...Be more patient!

Life, All life requires T I M E.
To begin,
Grow,
Develop,
Change,
End...

And YOU are life.
Take time.
Use time.
Accept time.

Time is good

> Healing
> Constant
> Secure
> Stable
> Changing
> Continuous
> Fresh
> New

Your best friend.

UNIVERSAL LAW/PHYSICAL LAW...
Numbers 1 + 2...
Choice,
Change.

Breathing
Progressive Relaxation
Walking and Other activities

Breathing

Breathing is easy until you begin to notice it. Notice your breathing, but do not attempt to control it.

This can be a hefty idea, for, once you begin to notice and observe your breath, something inside may have you sigh, that is, to breathe in deeply and let it out in a quick short burst! This is a good thing.

The body naturally sighs to refresh the brain. One breath in, a pause, then a release out, clears the mind. Think of a time you were running late for an appointment or stuck in traffic going to work. At a certain point, realizing you will be late, you let go, take a deep breath and say; "Oh well!", and settle into the situation. The more tense your breathing, the harder it is to release, let go of an experience.

Think of a time you were in pain...
Breathing can be labored, shallow, quick...
Heightening every nerve in the body. Once
you relax, starting with a single breath in and
out, you gain control of the situation, or
amount of discomfort experienced.

So, Okay, notice your breath, as it goes in and
out. Become comfortable simply observing the
natural rhythm of your breath.

Give yourself some time, some room to learn
how to simply observe your breathing,
Without controlling it.

Now, observe your breathing without thinking
about it. Simply allow you attention and focus
to this particular moment.

All other things that you need to attend to will
wait 5 minutes, sometimes 7 minutes, even if
strategically timed, 20 minutes. To just notice
breath without anything interfering, no things.
No reason thoughts can distract you from allowing this special time with simply yourself.

Believe it or not, you have just performed on act. You have also changed a habit you may not have been aware of; Thinking non-stop!

To give structure to breathing, practice taking a breath in through the nostrils while feeling the breath expand your belly, then at the bottom of your lungs, the middle and finally at the top of your lungs. Hold it for a moment, then release through the mouth, blowing. Again, practice. Balance filling these sections. Pushing out the belly a little, as though air is filling this space gives room to fill your lungs more completely. It moves stale air out also allowing for more ab-sorption of oxygen, feeding the entire body. Clearing the mind. Without air we cannot live, it is a nutrient. The brain needs this vital source.
When the brain is happy and satisfied, you are comfortable and have a sensation of well being.

Combine the above exercise with counting slowly up to 7 as you draw in a breath through your nostrils, pushing the belly out to fill your lungs systematically. Hold your breath to a count of 4, then release from the mouth on the count of 7.

You may increase the pause to 7 once you have practiced and mastered breathing.

Do this at first 3-5 times.
Notice how you feel or how your day goes afterwards. You may begin to find things that upset you may not be so important, or a solution comes to mind as to how to change the situation, or dealing with challenges.

It is totally amazing on how a simple exercise can positively affect many levels of our lives. Many famous people would take a 'nap' during the day, or the phrase; "I'll sleep on it" comes from the recognition that dropping a problem or issue for a short time, essentially walking away from it, allows the brain, the mind to organize, often producing an answer to a problem or challenge once we relax.

This technique is very portable, it is with you everywhere you go! Takes moments yet yields so much.
Remember it.
Practice it.
You can only prosper from it.

Progressive Relaxation

This exercise requires setting aside some time, at least 20 minutes to begin with. As you become proficient , a few minutes, even the thought of relaxing will allow you to completely enter a place of comfort physically, mentally and throughout your entire being.

However, exercise is exercise, and takes a little dedication and practice. Once you add a new routine to your life, after a while, it becomes second nature.

Begin by finding a comfortable position either lying down or in a comfy chair. If you choose not to turn off your phone, allow voice mail to catch the call, and let it be okay. Dedicate this time solely to yourself, choose to avoid any distractions. Decide this is a gift to yourself, uninterrupted.

Loosen any tight clothing, and allow yourself to shift around until your body becomes so relaxed you become still. There is no wrong way to do this exercise. It is a learned skill. Focus your attention to your breath for a moment. Breathe in slowly and deliberately through the nostrils if comfortable, pause, and release through the mouth. Do this 3-5 times.

Close your eyes to prevent any environmental distractions. Move your attention and imagination to your feet, the toes. Pick one toe, the large one on either foot and move it up and down. Then relax it. Relax every tissue, tendon and muscle. Move your attention to the next toe, flex it if you want, or pretend your breath is going into it and as the breath releases, it releases any tension, stress or strain in this toe, and so on... Move your attention to the balls of the foot, into the heel and ankle. Flex the heel and ankle, noticing the difference of tension and release, then moving up into the calf then knee, relaxing every tendon, every muscle, every tissue, down to the cellular level. Be aware of any pressure and pretend to breathe into it or flex it, then let it go.

Move along the body up to the thigh and hip, along the side of your belly into the ribcage. Tell these portions of your body to relax, be at ease.

Remind yourself if necessary that you do not need to be anywhere but here. Focus all of your thought and attention on letting go of physical stress, tension and frustration.

Your breathing has naturally slowed and is rhythmic and paced. Bring your attention to the shoulder and neck. Move down the upper arm, elbow, wrist and down through each finger. Imagine tension draining out of your fingertips like a faucet opened, releasing every stress, strain and thought. Use your imagination to see, feel or hear the sensation of stress, strain, physical discomfort draining from your entire body, with the rhythm of your breathing. Imagine as you inhale the breath is circulating throughout your entire body, soaking up any aches, pains, any thoughts that are not focused upon simply relaxing. As you exhale allow this to drain from your fingertips. Move attention again to the neck and up along the side of the jaw. Open and close your jaw if you observe any tension here, then into the cheek and eye. Relax your head moving across to the other side, down to the ear and down the back. Focus your attention to the upper neck, feel the vertebrae moving along the spine, across the shoulder blades, feeling them part slightly, releasing tension, stress and strain.

Every muscle, every tendon, every tissue at ease and comfortable. Move down to the center of your back, the sides and into the lower portion, near the hips. Breathe into these areas, instruct it to relax and release, as though you are preparing to sleep.

At this moment, you may notice the difference in the sides of your body, one side tense, the other utterly relaxed. You may move your attentions to the large toe on the opposite foot, but usually the body will take the cue and relax totally.

Once this is achieved, any suggestions you want to give will take hold. The body at this state is in balance. The body naturally repairs damage at this level and will leave you with a sense of well being. Your thoughts and tensions held in the muscles, tendons and tissues releases and a clearing, a cleansing occurs, on a physical and psychological level.

When you are finished, instruct yourself that in a few moments you shall open your eyes feeling fully awake, alert and refreshed, in mind, in body and in all ways. If you are going to sleep instruct yourself that you will receive the best nights sleep you've had in a long time and that you will awaken refreshed in mind and body alike, in all ways, in every way.

You may want to record this exercise on a cassette or CD and pop it in a player or simply follow the guidance. The state of relaxation is the point.
It is the spacious present desired.
And if only a few moments are achieved, you have been successful. With practice comes mastery. With mastery comes control.

Walking and Other Activities

This exercise is not meant as a calorie burner!
It is a deliberate, attentive action to focus your
thoughts down to just one; the intentional act of
placing one foot in front of the other, and
moving forward. Begin in comfortable clothes
and shoes to prevent any distractions. Choose
a safe place to utilize this exercise, your yard,
home or familiar place. I would not recommend a mall unless it is devoid of people.

Stand erect and straight. Put your hands to the
small of your back, if it is swayed or curved,
shift your hips forward or place one hand at the
small of your back and the other on the pelvis.
Stand up a bit straighter and push the pelvis
back and buttocks in, feeling with the other
hand the curve flattening out. This is a proper
posture. Take in through the nostrils if comfortable, a slow inhalation, pause and then
exhale through the mouth blowing.

Do this 3-5 times. Allow yourself to let go of all thoughts for the period of time given to yourself for this exercise.

Begin with knees slightly bent. Focus your attention on every motion. Lean a little forward, notice the shift in your hips, raise the right foot and place your heel on the ground as you notice rolling off the heel and up on the ball of your left foot, eventually this is done in a flowing motion... carefully, mindfully feel your weight shifting over the right knee and foot as you place it slowly down, feeling the heel, ball of your foot and then toes completely make contact on the ground, the left foot is still in place, mid-stride, feeling the toes maintaining contact with the ground.

Focus on your balance as you practice this. Focus on the action, the movement of your body only. It's pretty difficult not too beginning this particular exercise! Continue with the left foot, moving slightly forward, placing the heel down first, notice the shift of weight on your hips and the right foot rolling from the heel up through the toes, not allowing the right foot to lift up into the next step until the left foot makes complete contact with the ground.

Practice a little. It is so natural for us to get up and move where we need to without even thinking about it. To bring all of your attention to the actual mechanics of taking a step totally keeps your thoughts on the exercise. As you get the hang of it you want to walk slowly and mindfully, focusing on every muscle, tendon and posture through movement. Remind your breathing to be slow and natural...

Bring your attention back to the breath as you fisnish the exercise. Take a few deep breaths in and out. Instruct yourself that you'll be awake, alert, well in mind, body and in all ways.

My favorite "walking" exercise is scrubbing pots. Yours' could be anything, be it mundane such as washing the dishes or an intricate pro-ject, focus is the goal. Simply practice narrow-ing your thoughts and actions to exactly what engages you. Do not allow lists of things to do, to remember, and woulda, coulda, shoulda's thoughts not directly related to the task at hand, that want to entertain you.

As thoughts drift in and out of your attention, gently bring thought back to the task. Choose to not comment or judgment, like it is the 25th time your mind wandered off. It is part of the practice, that is why I suppose it's called practice, otherwise it would be called mastery...

Remember to be gentle with yourself, choose to proclaim progress. Many times se see what we want and haven't manifested yet, like shadow boxing.

All of these exercises perform the same thing: Sustained, intentional focus and attention. It allows you to remove clutter from the mind and the thought process. Just as humans require sleep to function properly, we need to clear the mind to function at our potential. Such as food nourishes the body, breath feed the brain and blood, down to the cellular level. The only known side effects of these exercises are a sense of well being, relaxation and Optimism.

About the Author

Kate Ellis, is a Certified Clinical Counseling Hypnotherapist, in practice near 24 years specializing in a broad spectrum of Anxiety Dis-orders. Kate's private practice, The Healing Quest, is dedicated to assisting clients with all expressions of anxiety, not limited to panic attacks, public speaking, ocd, pts & ptsd, social anxiety, insomnia, procrastination, depressive dis-orders and addictive issues, (people, substances, food) and pre-surgical hypnotherapy reducing significantly hospitalization time and recovery.

Kate has taught at Scottsdale Community College in Arizona, and was an instructor at Morraine Valley Community College and St. Xaviers University in Illinois.

Kate teaches a variety of courses including Personal self-development, Creative Visualization, Self-esteem, Assertiveness training, Self-Hypnosis along with Behavior Modification including; Anxiety/Panic Attack and Phobias, Stress & Pain Management.

Play and meditate on this word search puzzle. Solve it by encircling word-lines listed below grid; words are found as listed in every linear direction: up, down, backward, diagonal. Cross off word-lines found (above & below) until completed.

Kate Ellis www.empowerpuzzles.com

```
D E L L I F E B O T Y D A E R Z Q
Y P L U O S R U O Y N I K K R V S
E P D     W U A       V W E L L
H J         E         D A V R
O K                   I D G D
Q U                   O Y D Z
U R                   V T Z T
Y Q                   A O G R
U W                   S B V A
Z O Q                 P I E P E
I R Y                 L E K T H
E M M T               K X R I U R
A V U F N           W F Z E N W U
M E J R U O         R H B N H D U O
O G Z B B R D   O I T K V T L R Y
T H E R E I S A C A N D L E E T N
Y O U F E E L I T O E H P W D A I
```

There Is A Candle   In Your Soul

In Your Heart   Ready To Be Filled

Ready To Be Kindled   You Feel It

There Is A Void   Don't You

12/30/2011 @ 2310

9 780985 048372